965 EB

7 00

A Quayside Camera
1845–1917

A Quayside Camera
1845–1917

BASIL GREENHILL

Director of the National Maritime Museum

WESLEYAN UNIVERSITY PRESS
MIDDLETOWN, CONNECTICUT

To: P.A.B.

Library of Congress Catalog Card Number: 74-20469

Published in Great Britain by David & Charles (Holdings) Limited
Printed in Great Britain
First American Edition

ISBN: 0-8195-4088-9

Contents

List of Illustrations

The illustrations in this volume are reproduced by courtesy of the following:
National Maritime Museum: 1, 2, 3, 4, 5, 8, 15, 16, 17, 21, 22, 23, 25, 26, 27, 28, 29, 30, 31, 37, 38, 39, 40, 41, 42, 44, 45, 46, 47, 49, 50, 51, 54, 55, 57, 58, 59, 60, 61, 62, 65, 67, 76, 77, 78, 80, 84, 85, 86, 88, 89, 92, 93, 94, 95, 97, 102, 103, 104, 105, 106, 112, 116, 119, 121, 122, 125, 130, 133, 134. Basil Greenhill: 6, 7, 14, 20, 36, 48, 52, 53, 56, 64, 68, 79, 100, 126, 129. Captain W. J. Lewis Parker: 9, 12, 69, 70, 71, 73, 82, 83, 90, 91, 96, 101, 111, 127. Gillis Collection: 10, 87, 108. Mystic Seaport: 11, 18, 19, 32, 33, 34, 35, 81, 98, 118, 120, 124, 128. Reece Winstone: 13. Mariner's Museum, Newport News: 24, 72, 99, 114. Grahame Farr: 43. Robert Weinstein: 63, 74, 75. Public Archives of Canada: 66, 115. Cyril Staal: 107. Smithsonian Institution: 109, 110. H. Oliver Hill: 113. Official US Navy photograph: 131.

Introduction

This book is about two things which fascinate almost everybody. It is about men and women and the lives they lived and the world around them in the seventy years before the First World War, an age so close and yet so very different from our own. It is also about ships, and inevitably, from the period it covers, partly about sailing ships—the most beautiful and the most dangerous vehicles of transport developed by man. It comprises 134 photographs with descriptions of each one. The great majority were taken with cameras set up on or near quaysides on either side of the Atlantic between 1845 and the entry of the United States into the First World War in 1917.

This was the period in history when water transport services were at their most complete, when it was possible to ship goods to almost anywhere in the world on water where vessels could go. It was also the period when, although the steamship had been thoroughly proved, cargo-carrying sailing ships developed remarkably on both sides of the Atlantic in a sudden final spurt. They developed from wooden vessels of two or three hundred tons fitted with very complicated and flimsy arrangements of sails descended from those of the ships of preceding centuries to new types of ships altogether. The typical sailing vessel of the end of the nineteenth century in Britain was a huge four-master built of steel and carrying perhaps 3,000 tons of cargo, much more than her predecessors, or, at the other end of the scale of size, a wooden schooner or ketch carrying less than 200 tons, with very much simpler rigging than the vessels of fifty years before. In the United States and Canada equally big changes took place, in some ways even more revolutionary. Here the old wooden ships were first developed into huge vessels, rigged on traditional lines, and used especially in the trade back and forth around Cape Horn between the east coast and the west. Then, after the Civil War, more and more big wooden schooners were built, first with three, and then with four, five and six masts until these remarkable vessels, which bore no resemblance at all to the ships of thirty years before, became the typical American merchant sailing ship.

During the period covered by this book the steamship developed equally. At its beginning the *Great Britain*, the first modern powered ship, had just been launched. At its end liners so huge and sophisticated that they were nicknamed 'travelling palaces' were on every main passenger route and the steam-driven cargo vessel was the normal means of sea transport.

As for the navies, at the beginning of the period the great majority of ships in the navies of Britain and the United States were little different in appearance from those which had fought one another in 1812. At its end they had abandoned sails altogether and comprised fleets of steel steamships capable of hurling tons of high explosives over the horizons.

Of course, with all these changes the quality of human life at sea, though it remained very rough by modern standards even at the end of the period, also changed very greatly for the better. Nowadays we would consider the conditions for passengers and crew in the wooden sailing ships of the '50s completely intolerable, those of 1910 reasonably good and for first class passengers very good.

Another important change took place in the period covered by this book. At its beginning the United States merchant shipping industry was deeply involved in international trade; American sailing ships were in almost all the world's harbours. But with the opening up of the west and other developments, opportunities ashore for both capital and men were too great for either to continue to involve themselves on a large scale in maritime affairs so, as the sea power of Britain grew with her industrial expansion, that of America declined relatively. By 1870 Britain already had six times as much cargo-carrying tonnage in foreign trade as the United States. It is this disparity which has led to the absence of photographs of United States steamships in foreign trade in this book.

But apart from the phenomenal development of the big schooners and the huge paddle steamships which carried passengers on the coastal routes of North America, there were so many specialised maritime activities going on in the United States and Canada—whaling, deep-sea fishing, shipbuilding, the lumber trade, the coastal trade among many others—that there has been no difficulty at all in finding examples of the work of quayside cameras in North America. It was a great pleasure to make the latest of numerous trips across the North Atlantic to assemble the material from which the selection of North American photographs—more than a third of the total in this book—was made. In the course of collecting them I was able to visit again a number of harbours depicted here and to renew old acquaintance with some favourite places, especially 'Down East'. A photograph of the *Great Britain* in the National Maritime Museum and reproduced in my book *Steam and Sail in Britain and North America*, taken by Fox Talbot shortly after her launch in 1843, was very probably the first photograph of a ship ever taken. Thus fortunately for people interested in the fascinating subject of the maritime history of the nineteenth century, the use of the camera on the quayside is almost as old as the camera itself. Because of this the principal source of photographs in this book, the historic photographic archive of the National Maritime Museum at Greenwich, London, is remarkably comprehensive. For the American and Canadian photographs which have been assembled here I am most grateful to the Maritime Museum at Mystic, Connecticut, and to Waldo Johnston, its Director; to the Mariners' Museum at Newport News and to its Director, my old friend Bill Wilkinson; and especially to Captain W. J. Lewis Parker USCG (Retd), whose profound and scholarly knowledge of the history of New England shipping in the late nineteenth century sets standards few of us who work in this field can hope to emulate.

In preparing the descriptions of the photographs I have tried to avoid the use of more than the minimum of technicalities, but the historic and now dead language of sailing ships cannot be entirely avoided in a book which deals with this period. So I have had to use a few of the terms by which ships were generally described in the second half of the last century—brig, schooner, barque or bark. The sketches on page 11, taken from two contemporary manuals of seamanship, illustrate these terms.

I hope that this book, with its glimpse of a vanished world finally destroyed in Britain and to some extent in North America by the First World War, will whet the appetite of some readers to go further into this fascinating subject of the history of mankind's encounter with the sea. For anyone whose interest is stimulated, a visit to the National Maritime Museum at Greenwich, the world's largest, most comprehensive and most modern museum of its kind, is an experience in itself. At Mystic, in Connecticut, Newport News in Virginia, Salem in Massachusetts, Bath in Maine, Halifax in Nova Scotia and Port Hill in Prince Edward Island, Canada, to mention only a few of the North American institutions with which Greenwich is closely linked, there are splendid maritime museums, each specialising in some aspect of nineteenth century maritime history.

BARK OR BARQUE

BARQUENTINE

BRIG

BRIGANTINE

FORE & AFT SCHOONER

TOPSAIL SCHOONER

11

The First Photographs

1   The above photograph is one of a group by the Rev Calvert Jones in Swansea in the early and middle 1840s which were quite probably the first photographs ever taken of ordinary merchant ships. They show small wooden vessels with wooden masts and spars and natural fibre rope rigging which are nearer to the ships of the seventeenth century than they are to the great steel square-rigged sailing ships, the huge American wooden schooners and the steamships of the end of the nineteenth century. Yet these were typical merchant ships of the 1840s, the vessels that carried the products of the great industrial expansion of the period, and in which thousands and thousands of people travelled to the United States and Canada in the great mid-century migration across the Atlantic from Britain. The ship in the centre of the photograph is a new vessel, the barque *General Sir Willy Nott* of Swansea, built at Sunderland in 1845. The lines of gunports are painted on the vessels' sides to make them look formidable though they were, in fact, not armed—a reminder of the disturbed centuries of privateering and piracy which had come to an end only twenty years or so before this photograph was taken.

3 (opposite)   This photograph is included since it gives a good view of the hull and deck arrangements of one of these typical merchant ships of one hundred and fifty years ago. This brig (technically she is a snow, but this is a matter of small detail) is perhaps sixty or seventy feet long. When this photograph was taken the first regular trans-Atlantic steamship services, conducted by wooden paddle steamers, had just started and the first modern ship, the great iron steamer *Great Britain* now preserved at Bristol, had just been launched; but this little brig was far more typical of the merchant ships of the period than any of those exceptional vessels. No name is visible on the brig's bow for the good reason that the requirement to show the name on the bows did not become law until many years after this photograph was taken.

12

2   This is another of the remarkable Calvert Jones photographs. It has something of the texture and quality of an etching and it is superbly composed. The vessels lie at angles on the mud of Swansea Harbour at low tide, secured to moorings, for this was long before the docks were built. Again the vessels shown are of great historic interest. The ship nearest the camera rigged as a brig is the *Mary* of St Ives. She was only about seventy feet long, yet notice that she has windows in her transom which is a miniature of the *Victory*'s great stern. Those windows served to light her principal cabin. Small as she is, the *Mary* is again very typical of the small wooden sailing vessels which carried thousands of emigrants from Britain to North America between 1820 and the 1850s. Four other vessels can be seen, the nearest is the *Liberty* of Teignmouth, built in 1823, so this photograph takes us back more than 150 years. They are all about the same size as the *Mary* but are all rigged as schooners. About the time this photograph was taken the change from the complicated square rig of vessels like the brig to the much simpler schooner rig, imported from the United States, was beginning to take place in parts of Britain.

4　Taken in the 1850s at Ipswich in Suffolk, ten or fifteen years after the first three photographs, this photograph shows two sailors sitting on the quayside, while alongside the quay lies another small brig very like the vessel shown in Plate 3. Technically this photograph is very interesting because it shows in detail the way in which sails were stowed —this changed later in the century. A movable section has been lifted out of the bulwarks—that is the planked-in rails around the vessel's deck—to enable cargo to be loaded or discharged more easily. Although this little brig has painted ports like the vessel in Plate 1, they have become more conventionalised and no one could mistake them for a line of guns. Nevertheless they continued to be used as a decoration for forty years after the photograph was taken.

5　It was cheaper to equip a vessel with the simpler rigging of a schooner than the complex sails of a brig and cheaper to operate her as well, so after about 1840 the schooners developed in the United States in the eighteenth century began to come into increasing use in Britain. This photograph, taken at Ipswich in the same era as Plate 4, shows men carefully posed on the beach (remember all these early photographs must have been taken on home-made wet plates which required quite a long exposure) with a schooner lying at a wooden wharf in the background. She has very round full bows and would push a great deal of water in front of her as she sailed along. She is lying near the site of Clements' shipyard and the buildings in the background on the extreme right were Cobbold's Brewery, demolished in the 1890s.

6   So far we have not seen what these brigs and British schooners, built perhaps a century and a half ago, looked like when they were at sea with their sails set. A photographer who had his camera set up on a quayside one summer's day in 1862 had the great good fortune to catch a schooner on the left and a brig on the right leaving harbour under sail. Though both were sailing the breeze was gentle and the light evidently excellent so the photographer was able to give the very minimum of exposure. The schooner moving across the field of vision of the lens is very slightly blurred; the brig, moving directly away from the camera, is very clear and sharp. The differences between these two classic kinds of early nineteenth century sailing ships are obvious. The brig is a tall, stately, handsome, two-masted miniature of a Nelson line-of-battle ship, the schooner with plenty of square sails, like those of the brig, on her foremast for running before the wind, is actually primarily dependent on her gaff sails, like those of the old-fashioned yachts now called 'old gaffers'. Her rigging is much simpler than the brig and needs a smaller crew to handle it.

7   The location of this quayside scene, apparently a transaction involving the sale of fish, is not certain but it may well be Brixham in Devon. There is a lugger from Rye in Sussex in the background with the very early registration number 3. In the 1860s when this photograph was taken, Rye luggers were still working far down the Channel and sometimes selling their fish in Westcountry ports. There is also an early iron steam coaster or fish carrier vessel rigged as a kind of schooner, in the middle of the picture. As so often in the fishing ports one hundred and more years ago and indeed until the First World War, in this photograph women appear to be playing an active role at the first of the several stages of buying and selling which lie between the fishermen and the ultimate consumer. That quite a long exposure was needed for this picture is shown by the movement of some of the figures and the ghostly appearance of the basket on the left arm of the gentleman in the dark suit and top hat.

8 The brig *Edward* was built at Workington, Cumberland, in 1797, only fourteen years after the end of the American Revolution. This photograph was taken at Workington more than a century ago while she was discharging a cargo of lumber by means of a tackle slung between her two masts. The *Edward* was eight years old when the Battle of Trafalgar was fought, eighteen years old and already well towards the end of a natural working life when the War of 1812 came to an end, yet she survived to be thought well worth photographing fifty years later. The work of discharging has stopped for the purpose and the men employed on it are standing in a row on the quayside.

9 In August 1869 the shipbuilders Peirce & McMichael of Chelsea, Massachusetts, launched the big wooden sailing ship—technically a three-masted full-rigged ship—*Comet*. She was 178 feet long and of well over 1,000 tons—by far the largest vessel to appear in this book so far. A photographer was there to record her just before she was launched, towering up on the building slip and dwarfing the men who built her. Square-rigged ships as big and as fine as this were built in small communities all around the coasts of New England in the great days of the 1850s and 60s and even the 70s. At this time the shipbuilders of the United States had developed the big wooden square-rigged sailing vessel to a very high pitch of speed, efficiency and beauty, brought about by the opening up of the Californian trade and the big timber stands of New England.

10　By way of total contrast, this superb photograph was taken on the beach at Porthgaverne in North Cornwall, England, at about the same time as the last one, or perhaps a little earlier. It shows two coasting smacks—small single-masted sailing vessels which carried a good deal of the coasting trade of western Britain until the 1870s—one of them loading slates brought down from the nearby Delabole quarries in four-wheeled carts each pulled by two horses. The slates are being loaded by three separate groups working as a co-ordinated team. A group of men lift the slates from the carts and give them to a group of women stevedores, who pass them over the deck and down into the hold where they are stowed by a third group. The taking of the photograph was a very special occasion and some of the women have come up on to the foredeck, one of the men is waving his hat and cheering. Women stevedores were regularly employed to work on heavy cargoes at several places in western England in the middle of the last century. These vessels on Porthgaverne beach were in an exposed position should the groundsea work up and so they had enormously thick hawsers out to moor them. These were attached to special posts built into the vessels' sides at the stern. In the photograph they are visible through the opening in the bulwarks.

11 In great contrast again, this photograph was taken by a quayside camera in the hands of Stephen F. Adams of New Bedford, Massachusetts, in 1870, a year or two after the last photograph. It shows the wooden whaling barque *Massachusetts*, built at New Bedford in 1836. On the quays are some of the barrels needed to take the whale oil cargo produced by a successful three-year voyage in a vessel of her type. These ships, which laid the foundations, one way or another, of a number of modern American family fortunes, went out from Nantucket and New London as well as other New England harbours in the mid and late nineteenth century, but the chief whaling port of the days of the sailing ship was New Bedford, which in 1857 had 330 vessels in the trade. They sailed on long voyages to the Pacific where the whale fishery had been opened up, but never developed, by the British at the end of the eighteenth century. They sailed in pursuit of the sperm whale, hunting these huge beasts with open rowing boats from which they attacked with hand-thrown harpoons and lances in the manner immortalised in Melville's *Moby Dick*. The industry was an extraordinary survival from the seventeenth century into the age of photography. It produced oil for lamps, fat for candles and whale-

bone for numerous purposes now fulfilled by plastic such as collar stiffeners, but the life of the men who manned these ships was squalid, hard and dangerous, even by nineteenth century industrial standards. A sailing whaler contemporary to the *Massachusetts*, the *Charles W. Morgan*, is preserved intact at Mystic Seaport, Connecticut, where she is on public display with boats and whaling gear.

12   These pictures taken in the early years of photography end with a photograph showing a scene utterly remote from the world of the late twentieth century. It shows the little town of Waldoboro in Maine and the brigantine *Storey Clark* built by Edwin O. Clark in 1869. The cove is there and the site can still be located—in fact I went there and looked at it while I was writing this book, but everything else has changed. This little vessel, registered in New York City, probably sailed to many different parts of the world carrying cargoes of 300 or 400 tons for local consumption in the small places she visited. Goods were manufactured in small parcels and delivered direct to the district in which they were used and it paid to do business on this scale. Among the large sailing vessels built in these small New England communities, therefore, were many smaller ships, some of which were locally owned by shipmasters, school teachers, doctors, lawyers and farmers who participated directly at financial risk in ventures which often reached the other side of the earth.

Docks and Harbours

13   Quayside photographers often recorded picturesque small harbours and the people and ships which used them, but infrequently the big docks which made less obvious subjects for saleable post-cards.

   This photograph shows the historic Bristol Dock about the year 1865. The whole of this part of the harbour has now been bridged over and buses and cars stream continuously over the site of this pleasant waterway with its shipping. The drawbridge in this photograph was built in 1827 and lasted roughly three years after the photograph was taken, being replaced by another drawbridge. In 1891 a fixed bridge replaced that and the schooners could no longer go through to discharge their cargoes. As a schoolboy, however, I used to visit on board wooden sailing ships which lay discharging cargo just to the right of the right hand side of the picture. Bristol Docks are rapidly dropping out of commercial use for reasons obvious to anyone who has watched the tidal performance of the River Avon which gives access to them. Now the shipping is concentrated in new dock complexes at Avonmouth, some miles away on the shores of the Bristol Channel.

14 Loading and discharging cargo at Poole in Dorset, probably in the 1890s. The photograph was made by a time exposure and the man in the white shirt standing by the wheelbarrow moved considerably while it was taking place. Notice the two horses moving railway trucks in the centre of the photograph and the two-wheeled cart collecting coal from the coal depot, the horse busy with its nosebag. Judging from their black faces, the men in the immediate foreground are discharging a coal cargo. The vessels are the brigantine *Volunteer*, probably a vessel built in 1855 in Nova Scotia and owned in Dublin in the early 1890s, and the barque *Competitor* built at Boston, Massachusetts, in 1852 and owned in Germany in 1892. The latter has probably brought a timber cargo.

15 Grimsby in Lincolnshire is famous as a base of a great fleet of modern long-range motor trawlers and it was as a fishing port that it developed in the nineteenth century. This photograph shows another aspect of Grimsby's trade, cargo vessels, steamers and big sailing vessels, crowded into the port in the middle 1880s. A scene like this, common until the First World War, will never be seen again. The big square-rigged vessels have a section to themselves later in this book. The steamer in the foreground, the smallest ship in the photograph, is the *Bradford* built at Glasgow in 1865 and owned in Grimsby at the time the photograph was taken.

16   This jolly scene was photographed on board the *A. G. Ropes*, a magnificent American wooden full-rigged ship built at Bath, Maine, in 1884 and one of the two or three finest merchant sailing ships under the American flag in the late nineteenth century. She is lying in port waiting for orders to proceed to pick up her next cargo and the shore party of visitors is being shown around the crack ship. Behind them is the entrance to the poop where the ship's officers lived; the poop deck, the command position in a big sailing vessel, is above it. Captain Dave Rivers, the Master of the *A. G. Ropes*, is standing with his back to the camera on the left. The *A. G. Ropes* was one of the great wooden square-rigged vessels built in New England to meet the demand for ships to export grain from San Francisco to Europe, a trade which was very prosperous in the 1870s and 1880s. These vessels, known from their ports of origin as 'Down Easters', were very strongly built, fast yet economical and able to carry large cargoes. They were the last type of wooden merchant sailing ship to be developed in the United States except for the great schooners, which overlapped with them in time and which have a section of their own later in this book.

17   When a sailing ship was in dock a great deal had to be done to maintain her. Wooden ships were constantly being worked on by their own carpenters and crews. Steel and iron vessels had to go to ship repairing firms for most maintenance work, but there was constant cleaning and painting and working in the rigging going on all the time. Here the crew of a big steel sailing ship have brought down a sail, probably for repair, while the vessel is loading or discharging cargo. The length of the long snake of rolled up canvas represents the breadth of the sail and the length of the yard from which it is set. The fact that it is not bulky shows that despite its length it is nevertheless a relatively small, shallow sail, perhaps an upper topsail. Few people realise today how huge were the big lower sails of these great steel sailing ships.

18   This is the port of New Bedford, Massachusetts, at the height of the American sailing whaling industry, which was principally based there in the early 1870s. The vessel on the right hand side of the dock is the *Sunbeam*, a famous whaler built at Mattapoisett in 1856 and a real old world wanderer. The vessel bows on next to her has not been identified, but these stern and bow views together provide an excellent illustration of these full bodied and dumpty old whalers. Of course, they had no need of speed in their wandering voyages, their function was to carry the maximum amount of whale oil and other whale products and the mass of barrels in the foreground indicates just how much oil they often did obtain. This particular lot is stored on the wharf awaiting a favourable market; the owners, dressed in long-tailed coats and top hats, would from time to time visit the wharves to test and mark the barrels and assess whether the time had come to sell them. The vessel on the extreme left is a different class of vessel altogether, a cargo vessel, a fine wooden barque, typical of New England-built square-rigged merchant ships of the period.

19   The barrels which featured so large in the last photograph were not only important to whalers. Before the days of bulk tankers the barrel was essential for the transport of liquids. Some solid cargoes were also carried in barrels but, even more important, most ships' supplies, both solid and liquid, were packed in this way as well. The trade of cooper, the barrel maker, was extremely important to the whole economy of sea transport and to the operation of naval vessels at sea. In this photograph the quayside camera has caught coopers at work on the wharves by the whale dock at New Bedford, surrounded by the iron hoops of their trade. These men look as if they are breaking down barrels after the oil has been drained out of them, rather than making new ones. The whalers' barrels were, of course, not taken made up—they would have occupied far too much space—but in pieces which were assembled by the ship's cooper as they were required.

20   This very pleasant view of the quiet High Street of Bideford, Devon, was probably taken in the 1890s. It shows the quay in the background with a tall-masted ketch discharging cargo into carts by means of baskets slung on the end of a cargo gaff. Today, of course, both the quay and the High Street are filled with cars all day long but there is a sea-borne trade, recently increasing. German and Dutch as well as British motor vessels still discharge cargoes, principally of timber from mainland Europe, just where the ketch is lying.

21 This also is a Westcountry harbour. The schooner is discharging coal into the yard of a local merchant. The little girls, the one on the right almost totally submerged in her sun bonnet, appear to have brought down the lunch and the fish basket for the man in the boat. Both they and the little boys who are looking on are relatively prosperous children. They have boots and shoes and stockings and are wearing them. Before 1914 most local children in places like this went barefoot when they were outside school, except on Sundays.

22   This photograph is included because it shows a different aspect of the reality of a late nineteenth century port—a river with heavily industrialised banks, miles of railway sidings with steam cranes, miles of bleak industrial wasteland, which were as characteristic of the age as in a different way they are of ours and which were the only background and playground of far too many children like these two little boys. This quayside camera caught also two of the most famous small British sailing ships of the period, the wooden two-masted schooner *Isabella* of Barrow and her sister ship of the same fleet, the steel three-master *Result*. The *Result* is still afloat. She belongs to the Ulster Folk Museum and it is hoped to restore her to her appearance when this photograph was taken.

23   The South West India Dock, London, probably in the middle of the 1870s, shows a jumble of big square-rigged merchant ships and one naval vessel, HMS *President*, the hulk without masts furthest from the camera. The vessel lying next to her, slightly heeled over and without the upper part of her rigging is the *Sobraon*, a very famous emigrant ship in the Australian trade in her day. Another is the *Lincelles*, built in 1858 at Mulmein in Burma for a British shipowner in the eastern trade.

24 By the end of the nineteenth century the schooner had been developed in the United States and Canada into the principal type of big sailing ship in North American waters. This remarkable photograph, taken at Newport News in Virginia, records five of these huge vessels, two in dry dock and three afloat and they have from three to seven masts. They are, in order of number of masts, the *Sallie I'on*, three masts, the *Malcolm Baxter Junior*, four masts, the *Jenny French Potter*, five masts, the *Eleanor A. Percy*, six masts, all wooden ships, and the great steel *Thomas W. Lawson* with seven masts. The *Thomas W. Lawson* was the third largest sailing ship ever built, so big that Newport News was the only port of her regular trading places where there was depth of water enough for her to load a full cargo of coal to be carried to the ports in New England.

25   The export of salt fish to Europe where it was a most useful cheap staple food played a fundamental part in the history of Newfoundland and brought a miscellany of vessels from all the coast of the North Atlantic to her little ports. Photographs of Newfoundland harbours in the nineteenth century are rather rare. This one shows Harbor Grace; the steamer is the *Invermore*. The men are loading salt fish into her from a heap on the wharf, no doubt as part of a general cargo. The very small schooner in the immediate foreground is a typical local vessel. Newfoundlanders in the nineteenth century were noted for building these very small schooners, vessels which in the United States or Britain would have been rigged as sloops. The pole-masted ketch behind her is Danish and she has come all the way across the Atlantic to load a cargo of salted cod. Danish schooners and ketches were still crossing the Atlantic to load at these small Newfoundland ports after the Second World War.

Paddle Steamers

26 Steamships began as side-paddlers with simple low pressure engines of various kinds. Generally speaking two main types of propulsion developed, one on each side of the Atlantic. The British preferred the side-lever engine with rocking beams down in the lowest part of the engineroom to convert the up and down motion of the piston into the rotary action of the paddle shaft. The Americans adopted the walking beam, that is the rocking beam placed high up above the decks of the vessel. Soon supplanted in general sea trade and in fighting ships, the paddle steamer prospered on both sides of the Atlantic until after the First World War as a fast passenger vessel in sheltered waters and for certain kinds of towage work. Because their relatively simple engines and also the paddles could be seen working, paddle steamers have a peculiar fascination which still grips many people today and both in the United States and Britain paddle steamers have been preserved, at least two in museums. In Britain the paddle tug *Reliant*, illustrated later in this book, is preserved intact at the National Maritime Museum in a position in which you can walk her decks and visit the engineroom and see the crew's accommodation. In the United States the splendid side-paddle steamer *Ticonderoga* is preserved ashore at the Shelbourne Museum, Vermont.

By the side of a Devon river, shortly before the beginning of the First World War in Europe, this quayside camera has caught the moment of arrival at the quay of the local paddle steamer service in a flurry of foam and paddle-wheels. She is the *Kenwith Castle* built at Plymouth in 1914, carrying a small freight of passengers, many of them young women. Two of these little British paddle steamers are still afloat, the *Kingswear Castle* which belongs to the Paddle Steamer Preservation Society and the *Compton Castle* which is in private hands.

27 This jolly photograph was taken at Bridlington in Yorkshire, also shortly before the beginning of the First World War. It was evidently a perfect summer's day for being out on the water in one way or another. The local sailing fishing cobles are doing a booming trade with trippers and probably making more money in one afternoon than in an average week of fishing. They would nowadays be considered to be too crowded for safety and the young woman bending over the bulwarks on the port quarter of the *Dorothy*, the boat nearest the camera, is in for a rude shock if it becomes necessary to bear away from the next boat in a hurry. The paddle steamer is the *Frenchman* of Hull and she is also doing a booming business with visitors who are queuing up in great numbers to get on board her already crowded decks. The *Frenchman* was built at South Shields in 1892 as a tug and her appearance with passengers in this photograph illustrates another aspect of the work of paddle steamers in the age of the camera. They could and did double up as tugs and as pleasure steamers until tighter safety regulations ended the practice. In the 1880s, and probably later, an extra fare gave access to the bridge in some of these vessels and there are photographs extant showing the man at the wheel surrounded by crowds of passengers.

28 This delightful photograph shows a crowded paddle steamer in the 1890s on its way to the upper reaches of the Tamar, photographed by a camera on the Devon bank looking over towards the Cornish side just above Calstock. These steamers used to go right up to the head of tide water at Gunnislake where they turned round by backing their sterns into the entrance lock of the Gunnislake canal, which gave access to what was in effect a big floating dock of fresh water between steep banks notable for the number of mine workings on either side. These steamer trips were enormously popular and, after a long gap, they are as popular as ever again today, but now they are conducted by little motorships. The scene depicted here has changed scarcely at all in the eighty years since the photograph was taken.

29 This photograph shows Penarth Pier in Glamorganshire in the 1890s with a P. & A. Campbell White Funnel pleasure steamer embarking and discharging passengers. When there was no easily accessible harbour, the seaside pier was often the stopping place of pleasure steamers. This was especially so in the Bristol Channel, with its tides second only in range to those of the Bay of Fundy between New Brunswick and Nova Scotia in Canada. Here again it is obviously an ideal summer's day with a long queue for the steamer. The photograph has additional interest in the number of ships it shows in Penarth Roads, either sailing through or at anchor, some with sails set, apparently to dry. These were the days when the South Wales ports were still keeping large numbers of ships busy with the export of coal all over the world, while the schooners took it to northern France and around the coasts of Britain.

30 At the turn of the century this fine paddle steamer, the *Mona's Queen*, still retaining a sail on her foremast, was running a service from Fleetwood in Lancashire to the Isle of Man and back. She is shown here leaving Fleetwood, her decks crowded with passengers. She was built at Barrow in 1885 and served during the First World War as a troopship.

31 Of rather similar type to the *Mona's Queen* and very typical of the British paddle steamers of the late nineteenth century is the *Brodrick Castle*, built in 1878 but equipped with engines from an earlier vessel, the *Eagle* of 1864. At the time this photograph was taken she ran between Bournemouth and Swanage in the south of England. She is shown loading passengers at the pier in Bournemouth on a hot summer's day. These coastal steamers were very handsome vessels, comfortably appointed and steady in a rough sea. Often they provided not only pleasure trips but also a very convenient means of transport, especially in the Bristol Channel. One of the delights of a trip in them was watching the great pistons of the diagonal engines—yet a third type of engine used especially in coastal steamers in Britain —thrusting round the huge crankshaft on which the paddles were mounted. The smell of steam and hot oil was very distinctive.

32   The *Governor Andrew* was as typical of the latterday American paddle steamer as the *Brodrick Castle* was of the British. She was built at Brooklyn, New York, also in 1878 and sailed on the Boston Nantasket Line. She is seen leaving Boston crowded with passengers and her walking beam, high up behind her funnel, is very conspicuous. The British paddle steamers of the age of the camera made their passages either in relatively exposed waters in the summer months, or they were tug boats or, like the *Frenchman* (Plate 27), they carried out both functions. They were small or medium-sized vessels capable, as their performance as minesweepers in the First World War showed, of open-sea operation in bad weather. The American seagoing vessels on the other hand were mostly employed on fast regular services between centres of population, working often into very shallow berths, and they had behind them all the traditions of the luxury steamboat operation built up on the big rivers like the Mississippi and the Hudson. The result was an entirely different type of steamer from the British, well illustrated by those caught by New England quayside cameras and reproduced in the next five photographs. They were the solutions to a problem well put by a writer in the early years of this century 'You construct a six storey floating hotel with the length of two New York City blocks and the width of half a block', all this to operate on a draught of about fifteen feet at about twenty miles an hour, and yet to be highly manoeuvrable and, above all, quickly stoppable because of the danger of collision in crowded waterways.

33   The characteristics of the American coastal paddle steamer described in the caption to the last plate are very clearly illustrated in this photograph of the *Providence* of the Narraganset Steam Ship Company. The *Providence* was built in 1866 in New York City to a very high standard of construction. Her engine was the largest of the walking beam type in any steam vessel of the period with a cylinder of 110 inches in diameter and with a 12 foot stroke. She had 240 state rooms and over 300 berths and could, in fact, carry 840 passengers on a day trip. She was 360 feet long and 40 feet wide and her paddle wheels were 38 feet 8 inches in diameter. No wonder the small boys are looking at the huge structure with admiring interest.

34   This delightful photograph shows the smart steamer *City of Richmond* leaving what appears to be a harbour on the Maine coast with only a few passengers on board, but an interested audience of one in the rowing boat which has a covering resembling that of the 'Surrey with a fringe on top'. The walking beam is visible, as is very clearly the hogging truss structure without which these American steamers could not have operated. This truss comprised the twin girders which stretch as a low arch from the foredeck over the top of the paddle boxes on either side of the walking beam and down to the deck near the stern. Their purpose was to strengthen the long shallow trough of a hull which, from its very lightness of construction, would have worked and twisted and broken up with the heavy cargo of goods and passengers that these vessels carried if it had not had the additional strength provided by the hogging truss.

35   I have included this photograph of the *General Slocombe*, a New York excursion steamboat, because it shows the packed conditions in which passengers sometimes travelled in the days of relatively little regulation. Needless to say there were a number of disasters. Notice how even in this summer's day photograph the *General Slocombe* is heeled over on her starboard side. The two great dangers to these fast steamers were collision and fire. These shallow, flimsy steamboats had nothing to save them if badly holed in collision and carried very little lifesaving gear. When the *General Slocombe* herself burned up in New York Harbour in June 1904, some 1,000 people lost their lives. The potential horror of such a situation is well illustrated by this photograph.

36 The photograph of the *City of Richmond*, Plate 34, clearly shows the wheelhouse situated abaft the foremast from which these big side-wheelers were usually controlled. This photograph, taken in 1894, shows the inside of such a wheelhouse. These were the relatively luxurious conditions in which the quartermaster and the officer of the watch were carried in at least some of these vessels. Here, the man in the midship's window operates a small wheel through which the steam steering machinery is controlled. The huge wheels of the manual steering gear are locked and would only be used if the steam steering gear broke down. Steering by hand was very hard and a skilled job, requiring several men to do it. Even steering by steam with these broad shallow hulls required a great deal of experience. Big steamers like these were still running on the great rivers of Bangladesh in the early 1950s. I made many journeys in them and was occasionally invited to take the wheel and I found that to maintain anything like a reasonable course required great concentration and a lot of practice.

Packet Ships and Liners

37 Atlantic liners are a thing of the past, but passenger vessels like this one remain in service to take people to the continent and to the Channel Islands from mainland Britain. Nowadays they are smart motorships but this is a typical steamer of the last century. She is the *Stella* and she was photographed at St Peter Port, Guernsey, in the 1890s. Apart from the dress of the passengers the principal difference in the scene from its equivalent today is, of course, the fact that the boat has been met by a fleet of horse cabs and four-wheeled carts to take the baggage. The loss of the *Stella* on the Casquet Rocks in March 1899 was the worst disaster in the history of Channel Island steamers.

38 This is the *Gazelle*, another Channel Island service vessel, built in 1889. She spent the whole of her life running between Weymouth and the Channel Islands except when she worked as a minesweeper during the First World War. Note the masts of the sailing vessels in the inner harbour. The small vessel discharging luggage to the right of the photograph is probably an inter-Island steamer. This photograph was also taken in the 1890s.

39 Steamships continued to carry masts and sails for years after efficient engines had been developed. This photograph shows the liner *City of Rome* in the Mersey. She was built in 1882 and sailed in the trans-Atlantic services between Liverpool and New York and later between Glasgow and New York for twenty years. She carried 520 first class and 810 third class passengers and in 1898 she was used for the repatriation of 1,690 Spanish officers and men to Santander after the Spanish American War. During her days on the Atlantic she usually carried about 1,000 passengers on the westbound passages. In 1899 she stopped at Milford Haven on one eastbound voyage in order to land 120 members of Barnum's Circus which was on a visit to Britain. The circus went to London by train in order to get there quickly to keep an engagement.

40   How did people travel in the luxury liners and packet ships of the nineteenth century? Fortunately in the National Maritime Museum there are quite a large number of photographs of passenger accommodation and a book *Travelling by Sea in the 19th Century* has been published describing travelling conditions for all classes and how they changed as the century advanced. This photograph shows the first class saloon of the *Semiramis*, a liner of the 1890s, and shows a very high standard of luxury indeed. Note the pointed electric light bulbs, a product of the manufacturing process of the period.

41   This photograph shows first class accommodation in an unidentified liner. She still has oil lamps and no electricity so that the photograph was probably taken in the 1880s or even the 1870s. Notice the piano with its brackets for candles, the fireplace and the fountain. The swivelling chairs are designed for the easy use of people of both sexes in very formal dress. The capitals of the columns are delightful but the colours throughout are sombre and, to some extent at least, this probably reflects the difficulty of cleaning in a coal burning ship in the pre-vacuum cleaner age.

42   How were the thousands of passengers in an Atlantic liner fed in the era before the First World War? There was, of course, much less refrigeration than today and much more labour cheaply available, but the whole concept of convenience foods was unthought of. Food tasted on the whole either much better or much worse than today. This is one of the galleys in the *Mauritania* launched in 1909 and the first 26 knot holder of the Blue Ribbon of the Atlantic, the title given to the vessel on the route which made the fastest passage. Some of the items in this photograph, like the copper jugs and the Enterprise coffee mill, would be expensive collectors' pieces today.

Cargo Steamers

43 The development of the efficient, iron-built, compound-engined, screw merchant steamship in the early 1860s effectively meant that at last the days of the big ocean-going sailing ships were numbered. In fact, though, it was to be a long time—precisely 40 years—before big sailing ships ceased to be built and many steamships continued to carry masts, rigging and sails themselves. This was natural when vessels still had single screws and could be rendered helpless by a shaft failure or the loss of the propeller, which sometimes happened in the days when materials were not as dependable as they are now. This medium-sized steamer, heavily rigged as a brigantine, has met trouble of a different kind. She is the *Cousins Arbib* of London, a grain steamer; when coming up the River Avon to Bristol Docks in September 1883 with a full cargo she grounded when avoiding a moored barge. She was lightened by means of barges—the process was busily going on in the photograph—and floated off undamaged on the next tide.

44   This photograph shows a special type of rigged steamer, or sail and steam merchant vessel. It was taken at Harbor Grace in Newfoundland in 1888 and shows some of the local steam sealers in port. These were fully rigged wooden sailing vessels, fully powered as steamships. They were specially built for work in the ice and were enormously strong. This type of sailing ship with steam engines was developed for the British Arctic whale fishery which was conducted in the short Arctic summer, usually in the seas off Northern Canada. Many of them also made a spring voyage to Newfoundland and then joined in the annual slaughter of young seals drifting down the North Atlantic on ice carried by the Labrador Current. In due course many vessels of this type were built for Newfoundland owners and these 'wooden walls of Newfoundland' as they were called, because they were so well adapted to work among floating ice, were taken up by Polar explorers, notably Captain Robert Falcon Scott who used the *Terra Nova* on his ill-fated expedition to the South Pole and Admiral Richard E. Byrd who used the Dundee-built former Newfoundland sealer *Bear*, which had spent years as a United States Coastguard cutter, on two of his Antarctic expeditions.

46   The quayside camera which took this picture at Falmouth in Cornwall in the early years of this century caught a scene of great interest. The main feature is the steamship *Powhatan* of Liverpool, 2,599 tons gross, built in 1886 at Barrow. She has lost the masts and sails she probably originally had but she illustrates very well the kind of businesslike, utilitarian, steam cargo vessel which gradually replaced the big sailing ship in all the seas of the world as the nineteenth century drew to a close. She could carry more cargo more miles per year at lower total cost than the sailing vessel and, poor as they were by modern standards, the living and working conditions on board, outside the stokehold, were much better than in most of the sailing vessels of comparable size. So she attracted better officers and men. In great contrast is the beautiful three-masted clipper schooner *Susan Vittery* built at Brixham in 1859 for the business of bringing soft fruit back from the Azores for the British market. She was one of the most famous of all small British merchant sailing ships. Note the old GWR trucks and the steam cranes on the wharf, one of which appears to be loading the *Susan Vittery* with china clay.

45 (opposite)   The steamer *Alleghany* of Liverpool in dry dock alongside a small square-rigged merchant sailing ship of the type that the *Alleghany* and her kind were rapidly replacing when the photograph was taken. The photograph shows very well the full deep hull which gave these late nineteenth century steamers economic cargo capacity in addition to enabling them to carry adequate fuel—of course coal, hand fed to the furnaces—to compete in long range world trade. This photograph was taken at Falmouth, and the sailing vessel is lying in the very dry dock in which the barque *Palestine* lay in the early stages of the passage towards Bangkok with Joseph Conrad on board as a mate which Conrad subsequently immortalised in his story *Youth*. She is about the same size as the *Palestine*, called by Conrad the *Judea* in his only slightly fictionalised account of the passage and the vessel's loss by fire.

47   I have said that working and living conditions in late nineteenth century steamships were better than those in contemporary large merchant sailing vessels—except in the stokehold. The job of stoking great furnaces by endlessly throwing coal with shovels through the furnace doors, working in very high temperatures and in perpetual dirt from coal and ash, the whole working area moving at times violently up and down and from side to side, was one of the most hellish ever undertaken, even by nineteenth century working men. This photograph, though in fact taken rather later than any other in this book, gives some idea of what conditions were like in the stokehold of a hand-fired coal burner. The lift in the foreground was for heaving out ash, the disposal of which was always a problem.

Steam Tugs

48   Before steam tugs, or when they were not available, or when the shipowner or master could manage without the expense of hiring them, vessels were towed by their own boats or by rowing boats hired from the shore as shown in this photograph. Towing in this way was among the most arduous work regularly performed by seamen and boatmen. In this case the vessel is a Scandinavian brigantine being towed into a Yorkshire harbour with the flood tide by three men in a local fishing coble, while a member of the crew makes fast the square foresail—you can see him actually astride the foreyard. Notice the boat the brigantine is towing. She is an enlarged version of a yacht's pram, a Holmsbu pram built on Oslo fjord and much used as a ship's boat by Scandinavian vessels in the nineteenth century. It was probably from contact with these vessels that the modern yachts' pram developed in Britain and the United States. There is a splendid Holmsbu pram on display in the National Maritime Museum.

49　The first steam tugs operated at the beginning of the nineteenth century and tugs remain today essential to the management of big tankers and container ships in port. The sailing ship could never have developed into the great vessels illustrated later in this book if it had not been for the steam tug, nor could the passenger liners or big steam cargo vessels have developed either. This photograph shows the steam tug in one of its early forms, though by no means the earliest. These wooden paddle tugs of the 1830s and 40s are built like a wooden boat or a Viking ship with planks overlapping in the clinker or lapstrake tradition. This photograph, another of the remarkable Calvert Jones series of which there are examples at the beginning of this book, shows paddle tugs in Swansea at the beginning of the 1840s together with the sailing ships they towed in and out of Swansea harbour.

50　This camera on the quayside caught the paddle tug *United Service*, built at North Shields in 1871, bringing the brigantine *Anna* into Yarmouth on a roughish day with an interested crowd on the end of the pier watching the process.

This photograph graphically illustrates the great service tugs performed even with small and handy sailing vessels. The *Anna* would have been in some danger in entering the narrow channel between the piers in these conditions under sail, if indeed the direction of the wind had made it possible for her to enter at all.

51 Similarly these ketches would have had difficulty in getting down the Bridgwater River in
Somerset on the tide—and it is a very dangerous
river to be caught in because the steep-sided mud
banks can cause a grounded vessel to roll right
over as the tide ebbs—if the single steam tug had
not been able to take no less than seven of them in
tow together behind her. A tug in a river like this
could add greatly both to the use of the port and
the earnings of the vessels which regularly loaded
and discharged there.

52 This photograph shows what the operation
looked like from the tug. This screw tug, the *Coun-
tess of Jersey*, was built at Swansea in 1880 and in
the early years of this century was owned at Fowey
in Cornwall. Again, by getting sailing vessels out
of the harbour in contrary wind conditions she
made a good living for herself and performed a
valuable service to the seaport town. This photograph, taken from her foredeck looking aft, shows
her towing the big barquentine *E. S. Hocken*. The
Hocken is setting sail. There is a man on the foreyard loosing the foresail and she will shortly be
able to cast off the tow and have wind enough to
make her own way on the starboard tack.

53 This splendid quayside study of a later paddle tug was made at Bideford in North Devon in the 1880s. The *Privateer* of Swansea was built at Newcastle-on-Tyne in 1883 and from that year until 1895 worked as a tug at Swansea and in the summer months ran excursions with passengers across the Bristol Channel from Bideford in Devon to Tenby in South Wales. It cost five shillings to travel first class, which meant that you could climb on the bridge, a privilege you cannot buy on any excursion steamer today for any price. This is the top of the flood tide in the Bideford River. The quay today looks quite different as a result of widening shortly after this photograph was taken and because of the effects of the motor age.

54 This photograph was taken after 1917, but it shows a tug of the period before the First World War, unchanged since the time of her launch. This vessel, the name of which is not known, worked in Swansea and her whole appearance is that of a classic small steam tug of the 1890s or early 1900s. She is shepherding a small tanker through a lock and the crew, including her master in his shirt sleeves, are very aware of the camera on the quayside which recorded them in this one moment in their working lives.

55 This is the *Reliant*, the side-lever engined steam paddle tug now preserved intact inside the National Maritime Museum at Greenwich, where the visitor can go into the engineroom, walk the decks, look into the fo'c'sle and the master's and engineer's accommodation aft, which are displayed as if the crew had just gone ashore. She was built at North Shields in 1907 for service on the Manchester Ship Canal, from which she moved to the Tyne and from the Tyne to Seaham in Northumberland. This photograph was taken later than any other in this book but the vessel, apart from a change of name, is no different from when she was built—and she was an anachronism then.

Square-rigged Merchant Sailing Ships

56   The last quarter of the nineteenth century was the era of the big square-rigged merchant sailing ships, spectacular craft, some of them among the most beautiful vehicles of transport ever made by man. It was also the era of the big multi-masted schooners. The schooners were predominantly, but not exclusively, American and Canadian and they have their own place later in this book. The steel square-rigged vessels illustrated in this section were largely British. The big wooden square-rigged merchant sailing ships were American or Canadian-built vessels sailing under the British flag. The great steel sailing vessels of the 1890s are often thought of nowadays as typical merchant sailing ships, but of course they were nothing of the sort. They were, with the big schooners, the last form the merchant sailing ship took in technically developing industrialised societies and they lasted a very short time, about thirty years of the sailing ship's 3,000 years of history. The typical sailing ship of modern history is much more closely illustrated in the little brigs shown in the early photographs in the first section of this book. This photograph shows the *Pommern*, a typical British four-masted barque, built at Glasgow in 1903. She is still afloat, preserved at Marienhamn in Finland.

57 This very handsome vessel is the *Archibald Russell*, the last big merchant sailing vessel to be built in Britain. She was launched at Greenock in 1905 and had a long working career until she was broken up after the end of the Second World War. She is shown running with the wind dead aft. Notice how the square sails on the mizzen, the third mast, are filled and are doing most of the work. The rest of the sails are hanging almost flat. These great vessels sailed best with the wind on the quarter, that is over the side at the stern, when, with sails trimmed around (technically the yards braced round) every sail was filled and the maximum driving power developed from the wind.

58 Before the great four-masters began to be built in the late 1870s, ordinary big merchant sailing ships were iron and steel full-rigged ships—vessels with three masts, square-rigged on each, and such vessels continued to be built into the 1890s. This photograph shows the *Ardnamurchan*, built in 1890. She is sailing with the wind just on her port quarter with the yards

braced round a little. Notice the man at the open wheel with no protection against the weather. Imagine what conditions must have been like in that position in the sub-Antarctic, where these vessels regularly went on the long road from Australia to Cape Horn, a passage involved in one of their more profitable trades. American ships of the same period usually had wheel houses, which made steering a great deal less arduous and increased the safety of the vessel.

59 In the United States in the 1850s a new rig was developed from a British invention of the early nineteenth century—the barquentine or barkentine with one square-rigged mast and several rigged with gaff and boom sails. The sail plan proved on the whole very successful, it was much less complex and less expensive than the full-rigged ship or barque and more efficient than the big schooner, though she needed more men to sail her and she cost more to rig. This photograph shows one of the most successful barquentine rigged vessels, the *E.R. Sterling*, American-owned and sailing under the American flag. She was well ahead of her time in that she was the first merchant sailing ship to be equipped with a radio and she was fitted with an internal telephone system. She was a commercial success but came too late to have imitators. Should the merchant sailing ship ever be revived, in a world in which fuel is becoming more and more expensive, a version of the big barquentine using modern materials and techniques might well be one of the forms the new sailing ships would take.

60   The last British square-rigged merchant sailing ship to earn her living working from a port in the British Isles was a wooden barquentine—the *Waterwitch*. Much smaller than the *E.R. Sterling*, she had a successful commercial life from 1871 until she made her last voyage with cargo under the British flag in 1936. As the photograph shows, she was a handsome as well as being an historic vessel. She was launched at Poole in Dorset and for many years owned in Portsmouth. In 1910 she was sold to Cornish owners and registered at Fowey. She was later commanded by Captain C. H. Deacon, a great sailing ship master of an earlier generation who wore gold earrings and old-fashioned leather seaboots right down into the 1930s.

61 The camera that took this photograph was most certainly on the quayside. It shows a Norwegian wooden brig entering a British port under sail in the late nineteenth century. Technically speaking she is shortened down to lower topsails and the crew are in the act of taking in the main upper topsail, the spanker, and the main topmast staysail and the standing jib. The rest of the sails have been furled, a local boat is alongside putting men on board, one is in the act of climbing over the bulwarks on the starboard quarter. These men will probably assist in making the vessel fast when she reaches her berth inside the harbour.

62 Few steel sailing vessels of any kind were built in the United States and only one in Canada. This handsome four-masted barque, the *Atlas*, here shown on the port tack, was one of the American vessels. She was launched in 1902 at Bath, Maine; in the mid-nineteenth century Bath was the greatest shipbuilding place in the United States and is now the home of a fine Maritime Museum. In this photograph she has all sail set, and she is slipping along very nicely in a calm sea. She was an early oil tanker of a kind, built for the Standard Oil Company and carrying kerosene in cans.

63   The New England states and the maritime provinces of Canada were famous for their great wooden square-rigged merchant ships. The one shown in this beautiful photograph, the *St Paul*, is a classic example of these fine 'Down Easters' as they were called. She was built at Bath, Maine, in 1874 and in her youth in the Cape Horn trade from the north-east coast to San Francisco she had the reputation of being a very rough vessel to serve on board. According to the sailing ship historian Basil Lubbock, on one occasion a Baptist Minister was among the men shanghai'd on board in San Francisco. This photograph was made when she was an old vessel sailing in the canned fish carrying business on the West Coast. Notice the two men aloft on the mainyard taking in the sail and the mate leaning on the rail aft. Notice also that, unlike the *Ardnamurchan* in Plate 58, she has a wheelhouse, which among other features served to protect the helmsman from exposure to the weather and the possibility of being washed away by a following sea breaking on board.

64 This is the iron barque *Alastor*, built at Sunderland in 1875 for a firm which operated sailing ships in world trade out of Shoreham in Sussex in southern Britain. She is shown approaching harbour on a fine evening, sail is being taken in and her starboard bower anchor is ready to let go. She is a handsome vessel with a nicely curved stem, typical of hundreds of medium-sized iron and steel square-rigged vessels which carried on much of the world's trade in the 1870s and 80s.

65   The photographs so far seen in this section might give the impression that all big sailing ships at sea were always immaculately beautiful. This was by no means the case and the great majority of these vessels presented a much more workaday aspect than one might think from surviving photographs. This Norwegian barque, photographed in her old age, was perhaps more typical of merchant ships than the vessels in the earlier photographs. Built in Canada in 1862 and named *William Yeo* she was typical of the big Prince Edward Island built vessels. After years of Canadian and British ownership she became Norwegian. Notice the windmill pump used to keep pace with her continuous leaking and the master and the mate standing by the man at the wheel in the stern.

66 The trans-Atlantic lumber trade was of great importance in the development and peopling of the United States and Canada. In the middle of the nineteenth century scores of thousands of emigrants from Britain crossed the Atlantic to America in the empty holds of timber ships, which offered cheap passages to earn money on what would otherwise have been a voyage in ballast. The timber ship passengers made up a large part of the new population of the continent at that time. The ships loaded lumber in Maine, or more likely went up to New Brunswick or Quebec to take cargoes of 16 inch squared baulks, seen here loading through bow ports which were securely plugged when the hold was filled. The steamer alongside will take her cargo with her steam derricks over her side.

67 At the other end of the voyage small timber is discharged from a brig into sailing barges which will take it up the rivers on the flood tide to the lumber merchants in the waterside towns. The lumber business was of great importance to the areas of Britain from which the timber ships sailed, providing a means of emigration to many families in bad years of agricultural depression and bringing prosperity to shipbuilders and owners and employment to their workers and crews.

The Great American Schooner

68 The big American schooners with the contemporary great steel square-rigged vessels of Britain, like the *Pommern* (Plate 56) and the *Archibald Russell* (Plate 57) represented the ultimate development of the merchant sailing ship. The huge American vessels were not only beautiful, they were highly efficient for the work for which they were built, needing smaller crews for the tonnage of cargo carried than any type of ship, sail or steam, before them in history. Much of their work was done on the North American coast, but many of them crossed the Pacific to Australia and others crossed the Atlantic to Britain. It is quite wrong to think of them as coasting vessels, even though the long range coastal trade of the United States comprised their principal employment, for a very great number of offshore voyages were successfully accomplished by large schooners. In the year 1876 alone, for instance, no fewer than 233 trans-Atlantic voyages were successfully undertaken by American three-masted schooners and there was scarcely a European port from the Baltic to the Mediterranean in which they were not seen. This photograph shows the huge *Rebecca Palmer*, the first five-master to cross the Atlantic, lying in Fowey, Cornwall, where she loaded a cargo of china clay which she took to New York in thirty-two days, a good passage for a sailing vessel. Notice how her masts tower over the local shipping, even over the little town itself.

69   This schooner under all sail is the *Governor Ames* built at Waldoboro, Maine, in 1888, one of the first two five-masted schooners. This huge vessel had a drop keel like a modern racing dinghy or a shallow draught cruising yacht. She was in the long term a highly successful schooner, sailing round Cape Horn and across the Pacific to Australia. She once loaded a cargo of lumber at Puget Sound and took it round Cape Horn to Liverpool, England, in 139 days. Like that of so many of her sisters, however, the greater part of her career was spent in the coastal trade with coal cargoes from Virginia to New England ports, the trade for which she herself was built.

70   The *Governor Ames'* Puget Sound lumber cargo was loaded at Port Blakely, State of Washington. It was there that the only photograph known to have been taken on board this great five-master was made. It shows the two daughters of the master of the schooner, Captain C. A. Davis. In the original photograph the face of their mother can be dimly made out, peering through the window above the childrens' heads. The timber for Liverpool is being loaded over the stern of the vessel and slid right over the top of the master's and mate's accommodation in the afterhouse which, as in many of these great American-built vessels, is half sunk into the afterdeck. Notice the ironbound wooden driver mast and the chain standing part of the spanker sheet.

71 Mrs Davis was by no means the only wife of a master of one of these huge schooners to take her family with her to sea with her husband. Mrs James Alvin Flynn was photographed with her daughter, her husband, the mate and a couple of crewmen on board the three-master *Abbie G. Cole* of Machiasport, built at East Machias in 1891. Notice the fine yawl boat suspended on the davits over the stern. An example of a schooner's boat of this kind is preserved in the collection at Mystic Seaport, Connecticut.

72 The four-master *George E. Walcott*, built at Bath, Maine, in 1890 was discharging coal into big high-sided two-wheeled carts at Barcelona in Spain when this photograph was taken from the top of the afterhouse looking forward along the schooner's deck. Captain William F. Kreger is probably the man nearest the camera on the right. Notice the huge hoops with which the luffs of the sails were held to the masts, clearly visible on the jigger mast nearest the camera.

73   The handsome four-master *Charles D. Endicott* was becalmed when this photograph was taken. She has her main, mizzen and spanker sails set, but not the foresail, nor any of the topsails or head sails. Notice that she has an open rail all around her—quite unlike the solid bulwarks of the British vessels illustrated in this book. This is a fine, efficient, economical and beautiful sailing vessel and she represents very well the merchant sailing vessel at what was in many ways its highest form of development.

63

74 From the preceding photographs and text it might be assumed that these big United States schooners were peculiar to the east coast. This was not so. A number of these great sailing vessels were built on the Pacific shore. This photograph shows two four-masters, the *A. J. West* and the *Alert* at St Pedro, California, in 1911, discharging lumber from Oregon and Washington. Astern of them is the British barque *Formosa* which must have brought a cargo from British Columbia.

75 Incredible as it might seem, this was the only way of getting ashore from a schooner loading lumber on California's Mendochino Coast. The coast of California is notoriously without harbours and in some places too shallow to be approached by a big vessel. As good wire rope became available the problem was solved by the wire highline along which the lumber the schooners came to load was carried in slings. This photograph shows Captain Mitchell, Mrs Mitchell, the two Mitchell children, the mate and the children's nurse coming ashore from their four-master, which can be seen deeply laden with a huge deck cargo. The casualness of the men is natural, they grew up furling the gaff topsails of big schooners, but the women are no more concerned, though a squirm or a wriggle would send the little girl in her mother's arm 100 feet down into the log-filled shallows.

The Face of the Seaman

76, 77 and 78   These three young men were related and came from the Bideford area in North Devon and, as so many men from that place did in the nineteenth century, they followed the sea. They were photographed as far apart as their home town and Lima, Peru. They were of a good family which generated masters and at the time the photographs were taken, the first perhaps in the 1860s, the second in the 80s and the third early in this century, each of these men was a young mate or about to become one. They could hope to become masters in big ships owned by big companies and be lucky to make a few hundred pounds a year. Or they could become shareholders and masters in small local coasting vessels and lose in status perhaps, but with luck gain considerably financially. Nobody knows their names or what happened to them, but they will serve as the unknown seamen to represent the nameless host of simple men, largely cut off from the normal human life of the land, who sailed the ships whose photographs appear in this book.

79   And this is what a lucky man could become, a prosperous owner and master of small vessels. This is
a photograph of Captain David Sims who lived in the village of Saul at Gloucestershire, an inland village where the Berkeley Ship Canal joined the Stroudwater Canal. He owned a shipyard as well as ships
and he was master of several vessels including a fine schooner called the *Alert*.

80 The seamen before the mast in big sailing ships in the late nineteenth century were a mixed crowd, largely comprising drifting rootless men of many nationalities. They were superbly described in Joseph Conrad's great documentary novel *The Nigger of the Narcissus*. This photograph was taken perhaps ten or fifteen years after the bulk of the events which went into the making of that book. It shows the crew and some visitors on board the barque *Wasdale* of London, probably in the late 1890s.

81 These two young men are lazing in the folds of one of the great sails of a big American schooner, probably the *Maria O. Teel*. They were Irving Davis on the left, who was lost overboard from the *Teel*, and Stinson E. Davis, who lived to become a captain. The sail looks new and its luff is not attached to the mast hoops which lie loose on the jaws of the boom; perhaps these two were bending it—that is putting on the new sail—when the photograph was taken.

82   The New Bedford whaling barque *Charles W. Morgan*, now preserved at Mystic, Connecticut, sailed on a whaling voyage shortly before the United States entered the First World War. This was one of the last of the traditional voyages in the history of the great United States whaling industry. Her master was a veteran, Captain Benjamin D. Cleveland, and the night before he sailed he had this photograph taken in the *Morgan's* great cabin in the stern of the vessel. He is sitting on the leather sofa which runs right across her stern.

83   This composite photograph shows fifteen American Masters of big schooners, all in the employ of the Coastwise Transportation Company of Boston which was incorporated in 1903 and absorbed a big fleet of schooners built up by Captain John G. Crowley who became a manager of the new company and whose picture is in the centre of the group. These masters were short-back-and-sides men, looking in their best clothes less like the masters of big sailing ships as we imagine such men to have been than like contemporary business executives. The photograph must have been taken shortly before the First World War.

84 This scene was taken in dock, despite the fact that it looks as if the vessel is at sea. It is deliberately posed on board a big sailing vessel, a demonstration of the use of the old-fashioned log by three men, one dressed in Junior Officer's uniform, one, holding the log line drum, in working clothes but with his shore-going shoes on and one in full heavy weather gear of leather seaboots and oilskins of the old-fashioned type made by dipping cotton into linseed oil blackened with boot polish—these were seamens' oilskins before the days of rubber and plastic. This method of ascertaining the ship's speed, and therefore the distance run, was used from the sixteenth century until the beginning of this century. The principle was to time by sandglass the length of rope which ran out in fourteen or twenty-eight seconds. At the end of the line unreeling from the drum was a triangular piece of wood, weighted with lead so that it stood upright in the water as the line was hauled off the reel by its drag. When the line was checked a plug holding one of the lines securing the triangle would come out, the board would fall flat and be easily hauled in. The speed was measured from knots proportionately placed in the line to indicate miles sailed in an hour, from which derives the term knot as a unit of speed of ships.

85   These were the men who were masters and mates of the last generation of small British merchant sailing vessels. They all came from Appledore in North Devon. Though the photograph was taken about the year 1900, or soon after, a number of them have been identified by Captain W. J. Slade, the author of the two classic books on Appledore's last days as a home of merchant sailing ships, *Out of Appledore* and *Westcountry Coasting Ketches*. They are, second from the left, Hartree Harding, next William Gregory, in front Archie Ross, who sailed in schooners in the Newfoundland trade. The fifth person is William Screech of the ketch *Emu*, the man in the coat is Harry Sussex, a ship carpenter.

86   Daddy Johns, a ferryman who worked from Instow to Appledore across the River Torridge at the beginning of this century, carried all manner of men and women in the course of his daily work. These two ladies were members of a family which made regular summer visits to Appledore. To us they seem hopelessly overdressed for a summer's day, but then so does Daddy Johns himself with his characteristic Appledore 'frock' (the jersey with heavily worked shoulders), heavy serge trousers and soft hat. Like the ladies, he is almost certainly wearing long woollen underwear as well.

The Shipbuilders

87 The principal subjects of quayside cameras are inevitably ships and boats and the men and women associated with them as seamen, stevedores, pilots, passengers, boatmen, fishermen, fish dealers and in many other occupations. But the ships had to be built and in the period covered by this book many were constructed in circumstances that made their building a possible subject for a camera on the quayside or, at any rate, for one that did not move very far away. This photograph was made in 1877 near one of the old quays on the Gannel Estuary in North Cornwall. It shows the schooner *Louise*, about to be launched, with some of the men who built her around and on board her. She was built here by Thomas and John Clemens in a place from which it was possible to launch her only on the higher spring tides and then only sideways. Yet in this same place the Clemens and their father and grandfather before them built eighteen schooners, a ketch and a smack. The site was no doubt used because it was accessible from the land and perhaps there were no rent or rates to pay. The *Louise* had to be launched fully rigged because there was no fitting out berth. Like many other nineteenth century vessels, she had to sail straight away from her building place to pick up her first cargo.

88   This is another simple shipbuilding yard situated in the parish of Bere Ferrers in Devon, photographed from above Calstock Quay on the other side of the river in Cornwall. It shows the yard of James Goss of Calstock with the ketch *Garlandstone* under construction and two vessels under repair. Her keel, stem and stern post and half her frames have been set up and the jumble of wood, characteristic of any wooden shipbuilding yard anywhere in the world and a great deal more orderly than in fact it looks, comprises largely material which will go into her completion. The photograph was taken in 1905 and the *Garlandstone* was not finished until 1909. She was built on speculation to keep men employed in the yard in the intervals between repair jobs. She is still afloat and at the time of writing is being restored to her appearance at the time of her launch as an example of what these little wooden merchant sailing ships were like. She lies at Portmadoc in North Wales.

89   These are the men who built the ships at James Goss' yard on the banks of the River Tamar. They are at work repairing a wooden sailing vessel which has evidently been damaged in collision. The powerful man standing second from the right on the plank is James Goss, the master shipbuilder himself. He was a North Devon man, a seaman and a carpenter in big wooden sailing ships who moved to east Cornwall to join an uncle who had settled there and set up as a merchant and shipbuilder. He was immensely strong and a very able shipwright who was helped at the yard by sons and relatives, some of whom are among the men around him, and even by his daughters who helped him in the evenings after they came home from being 'in service', that is locally employed as housemaids. One of them told me a year or two ago that she could remember having 'to stand against father', that is help him with the rivetting of the strakes of wooden boats which he used to build in the evenings after the day's work in the yard was done.

90   In 1884 James M. Bayles & Son of Port Jefferson, New York, built the three-masted schooner *Nettie Shipman*. This is the *Nettie* on the slip with most of the work that had to be done before she was launched finished and this is the gang that built her with James M. Bayles himself on the extreme right. Many of the men are carrying the tools of their trades—there are two shooting planes, three caulking mallets and four adzes on the shoulders of men standing in the second row and an axe similarly held. Another axe is between the knees of the third seated man from the right. The caulkers with their narrow mallets—the ones shown here are unusually big and must have required men of strength to use them for hour after hour—drove the oakum, teased out natural fibre rope, into the seams between the planks of the vessels. Rammed home tight and tarred over it not only prevented leaking but also, by inducing tension into the structure, greatly increased its strength.

91   Eighteen years later, in 1902, the wooden shipbuilding industry, now almost dead in Britain, was still relatively thriving 'Down East' that is, in north eastern New England and maritime Canada. In that year Carlton, Norwood & Co built the great four-masted schooner *Edgar W. Murdock* at Rockport, Maine, a little settlement which has not changed a great deal around the harbour since that day. Here is a building gang alongside the partly finished vessel. The master builder, Chester Pascal, is seated fourth from the left in the front row.

92   For some reason photographs of iron and steel ships being built before the First World War seem to be much rarer than photographs of wood shipbuilding yards. This particular quayside camera was photographing the Hamilton Graving Dock in Belfast, Northern Ireland, at just about the same time as the photographer recorded Chester Pascal and his gang at Rockport. The scene, however, is very different. Two great coal burning reciprocating-engined single-screw steel steamships are fitting out in the floating dock, a third large steamer is in the actual Hamilton Graving Dock in the background of the picture on the right hand side. One the left the stern of another big vessel is visible under construction on the slipway. These are the sort of vessels which were the backbone of the vast British merchant shipping industry of the period and which had replaced the big steel sailing ships illustrated in an earlier section of this book.

93 A big shipyard building great steel steamships at the turn of the century had to have extensive supporting services to feed the slipways where the vessels neared completion. Foundries, boatbuilding sheds, block shops where the woodwork for rigging, pulleys, bull's eyes to lead ropes, etc were made, were essential. The carpenters' shops, where the joinery work for the cabins of passenger vessels and the crews' accommodation was made were often very large indeed. This photograph shows the shops at the yard of Denny Brothers of Dumbarton, Scotland, famous at the time as builders of medium-sized passenger steamers and of special paddle steamers for service on the great rivers of Asia. The carved panels on the right hand side of the photograph are for the first class saloons of small liners. This was the yard in which, under its previous owners, Scott and Linton, the famous British square-rigged sailing ship *Cutty Sark* was built. She is now preserved by the British Maritime Trust at Greenwich, London, adjacent to the National Maritime Museum.

94 Not all yards were neat, orderly, large-scale enterprises like Denny Brothers. This little yard at Hubbastone, part of Appledore in North Devon, was both a shipbuilding and a shipbreaking yard at different times, and sometimes at the same time. The extraordinary white painted cottage, the home of the shipbuilder's family, was called Delaware Cottage, and its story is worth recording. In 1881 Robert Blackmore who ran the yard bought the derelict brig *Delaware*. She had been built in 1863 on the shores of Egmont Bay in Prince Edward Island, Canada, by James Yeo, an emigrant from the Appledore neighbourhood and the greatest of Prince Edward Island's numerous shipbuilders. She was rotten, so Robert Blackmore broke her up, using timber from her and other vessels to build a home for himself. The top storey is the typical deck house fo'c'sle, where the crew lived in a small Canadian-built sailing ship. It was taken straight off the *Delaware* and was used as a boy's bedroom, keeping many of its original fittings. The house was demolished just after the First World War.

95 In the last century Prince Edward Island, Canada, was the building place of a vast number of wooden merchant sailing ships of all sizes, the majority of which on completion were sailed across the Atlantic and sold to British owners. The industry began in the eighteenth century and reached its peak during the war between the States in the early 1860s. This photograph, taken in 1892, shows the barquentine *Meteor* about to be launched from the yard of William Richards, a son-in-law of James Yeo who built the *Delaware*, at New Bideford in the Island. Most of the population of the countryside for miles around has congregated around the vessel's bows on this great occasion, while the yard gang appear to be mostly on board. The site of the yard can still be seen and a mile or two down the river the Government of Prince Edward Island has recently established an historical centre to commemorate the great shipbuilding industry. Notice the deckhouse fo'c'sle, on which two yard workers are standing, in the *Meteor*. It is the same sort of structure which was taken from the *Delaware* to make the top storey of the cottage shown in the last photograph.

96   This is a close-up of the huge wooden hull of the five-masted schooner *Jenny R. Dubois* about to be launched at Mystic, Connecticut, with an evidently excited crowd of men and women, a horse carriage and a long line of people wanting to go on board up the temporary stairs to see her broad decks and inspect her accommodation. The *Jenny R. Dubois*, like the *Edgar W. Murdock* in Plate 91, was built on the upsurge of an industrial boom which followed the Spanish American War of 1898. The consequent prosperity for shipping and shipbuilding lasted until 1904 and led with other factors to a great revival in the construction of big sailing ships for carrying soft coal from Virginia to Boston and other seaports of New England. For some years it looked as if the great days of sail had returned in the eastern United States, but in 1908 there was a disastrous depression which marked the end of the large-scale construction of sailing vessels in the United States, apart from a short wartime boom nine years later.

97 Shipbuilding yards on both sides of the Atlantic were very dependent upon repair work which, taken over the years, often made much more money than new construction. This is the Richmond Dry Dock in Robert Cock's yard at Appledore in North Devon in England about 1880 and shows two big sailing ships, one built of wood and the other of steel, under repair. Both are rigged as barques. On the lefthand side of the picture is the yard's sail loft; on the righthand, visible over the barque's fo'c'sle head, is the block and boat shop where the blocks, of which numerous examples are visible in the barque's rigging, were made. This photograph shows just how many blocks a big sailing ship needed and how necessary it was for a yard to have a special place for manufacturing them. The man in the soft hat standing nearest the camera on the lefthand side of the picture is Mr Hookway, the yard's foreman.

98   On the other side of the world at Aberdeen, State of Washington, USA, the great square-rigged wooden merchant sailing ship *Seminole* is undergoing extensive repairs. She, like the *Jenny R. Dubois* (Plate 96), was built at Mystic, Connecticut, but in 1865, and she was a typical big wooden vessel of her period, rigged as a full-rigged ship, that is, square-rigged on all her three masts. She was typical also of the big American sailing ships of the immediate post-Civil War period and operated in the trade round Cape Horn to the West Coast—the main route from coast to coast before the completion of the railway in 1869. She was considered by many of her contemporaries to be the finest New England-built vessel of her generation. On her maiden voyage she sailed from New York to San Francisco in ninety-six days. She spent her old age in the Pacific Coast lumber trade and no doubt this photograph was taken at that time. It shows her great mainmast being lifted up by sheerlegs. The big deckhouse fo'c'sle immediately forward of the mainmast was typical of New England merchant sailing ships and offered much better living quarters for the crew than did the fo'c'sles right in the bows of the ships which were favoured by British shipowners in this period. You can see one of these old topgallant fo'c'sles in the *Star of India*, preserved on public display at San Diego, California and there is a brilliant description of living conditions in one of them in Joseph Conrad's *The Nigger of the Narcissus*—perhaps the finest book ever written about life at sea in the late nineteenth century.

99   Plate 89 showed a great British builder of small wooden ships, James Goss of Calstock, Cornwall, at work in his yard. This photograph is a portrait study of Charles V. Minott of Phipsburg, Maine, who lived from 1826 to 1903 and who, during his working life as a master shipbuilder, was responsible for no less than thirty-four vessels from the brig *Nebraska* to the five-masted schooner *Marcus L. Urann*, a product of the last boom in wooden sailing ships at the beginning of the present century. This vessel was building when he died.

100 This photograph shows the launch of the *Wellholme*, a shallow-draught ketch fitted with lee boards to serve the same function as the centre plate in a modern sailing dinghy or shallow draft cruising yacht, from the yard of J. & W. B. Harvey at Littlehampton in 1916. She was one of a series of shallow-draught ketches built at this yard during the First World War which cost about £1,750 each—say 4,000 dollars. Today to reproduce they would probably cost about £100,000 or a quarter of a million dollars. Even at their low price they were taken by their purchasers on easy terms of instalment payments made as they earned their building cost.

No doubt because this photograph was taken in the middle of the war in Europe, there is no large crowd to see this vessel launched. The yard gang, the new owner and apparently his wife and child, are on board but the whole process is obviously being carried out with little ceremony.

101 This lively scene was taken in the yard of I. L. Snow & Co at Rockland, Maine, probably in the 1890s. It shows two fine three-masted schooners, the *Annie Ainslie* and the *Adelia T. Carleton* under repair with a two-master and a fourth vessel under construction. Like their British opposite numbers, these American shipbuilders depended upon repair work for much of their day to day living. The yard is a typical one; of great interest is the great piece of timber on the left with the number 90 painted on to it. It is the upper part of the stem of a schooner and it has either been prepared for the new vessel under construction or, more likely, for a repair job to be done on some vessel expected at the yard shortly.

Appledore Quay

102   Appledore, a town within the limits of the port of Bideford in North Devon, was the last place in Britain from which wooden sailing ships were operated commercially. Its closest North American equivalent was Lunenberg, Nova Scotia, though Appledore was concerned with carrying cargo, Lunenberg with deepsea fishing. Appledore had a great seafaring history centred around trade with Virginia, New England, and the Canadian maritime provinces and latterly trade with Europe and around the coasts of Britain. Appledore's last sailing vessel, the three-masted schooner *Kathleen & May*, did not cease to trade until 1960, about the same time as Lunenberg's motor schooners finally gave up dory fishing. This photograph shows Appledore Quay at the turn of the century. Notice the sails on the slipway, the water barrels, and the unpaved quay with its mooring posts. Of the three men talking, the man nearest the camera is Joseph Tanton, the centre man is Joseph L. Evans and the third Billie Fishwick, master of the ketch *H. F. Bolt*.

103 One of the local trades of Appledore in the late nineteenth century was the loading of gravel from the banks in the river into sailing barges aground on the banks at low tide. From these barges the gravel was transhipped into ketches and taken to Bristol or Cardiff or Barry where it was used for concrete making in dock construction work. The gravel was loaded into the barges by men with shovels, back-breaking toil for which they were very badly paid. Many barges were owned by publicans who made more money by selling their underpaid crews the beer which was essential for doing such heavy work. The whole industry is expressed in this photograph of William Lamey and George Tucker, bargeman, walking to the slip to board the barge at high tide. George Tucker carried the food and the beer in an earthenware jar. The barefoot boy behind in his father's rolled-up trousers is typical of the local social conditions at the turn of the century.

104 Two old smacks or small ketches lie off Appledore Quay at high tide while a lad sculls a boat past them with an oar over the stern. The boat is a typical Westcountry smack's or ketch's boat, only twelve or fourteen feet long, yet so burdensome that she will take nine lads in comfort and safety. Some of these boys may be going ashore from vessels moored off the quay and some are just along for the ride. Appledore boys were always out in boats, even when they were not working in them. The photograph was taken at the beginning of the century.

105   This superb study shows the barge *Secret*, built as a coasting smack at Calstock in Cornwall (Plate 88) in 1864, which became a gravel barge at Appledore in her old age. She is light, and her crew are in the process of putting her aground on a gravel bank so that she will dry out at low water. They will then load her with shovels, float her off as the tide rises again and sail her up to a berth where she will discharge her cargo, either for a local builder's merchant or into a ketch to carry up Channel for the building of Avonmouth docks, on the Avon below Bristol.

Fishermen

106   A quayside camera at Brixham, Devon, in the early 1880s caught DH 89, a smack-rigged Brixham trawler, tearing by, her sails filled in a good breeze. She is probably about to round up and anchor, like the other trawlers in the photograph and wait for the tide to rise so that she can get into the inner harbour. Some of her crew are forward in preparation for anchoring, the man at the tiller is clearly visible, as is the great beam of the trawl stowed, Brixham fashion, on her port side. These Brixham trawlers represented the big British sailing fishing vessel of the late nineteenth century at its best. In the 1880s the two-masted ketch rig, which enabled bigger and more powerful vessels to be built, was already becoming popular—see the vessel in the background on the right.

108 (opposite)   Fishing was men's work, but the cutting, sorting and salting was women's work and in the fishing seasons women workers followed the fleets and lived on the quaysides where they spent all day. This big group was photographed at Newquay, Cornwall, more than a century ago, at the height of the pilchard fishery, at that time passing through one of its periods of prosperity. The man in the top hat is probably the merchant who is financing the whole operation and who is the only man who will make very much money from it. The man with his hands in his trouser flaps is probably the foreman. Otherwise the only men in the photograph are those who carry fish across from the vessels. These women were rough and ready in their manners and any other male coming within earshot was likely to be subjected to a barrage of cheerful obscenities, invitations and personal comment.

107 Brixham trawlers used to fish far from home and during the summer months whole fleets would base themselves on distant ports for months on end. This was particularly true of Tenby in South Wales and the annual migration had the side effect that some Brixham men settled in Tenby and others took Tenby wives back to Brixham, so that a strong connection developed between the two towns. These trawlermen have come ashore at Tenby to sell their fish at the earliest possible moment, probably while their vessels are waiting for the tide to get into the inner harbour at the end of a week's fishing. The man in the two-wheeled cart which has been driven into the sea is loading fish he has bought straight from the boats, while some of the trawlermen are apparently simply taking the opportunity to stretch their legs after several days on board.

109 Whereas British sailing fishing vessels in the late nineteenth century were rigged as smacks and later as ketches, those which followed the great offshore fishery of eastern North America, both from the United States and from Canada, were rigged first as sloops and later as schooners. One of the earliest forms of schooner, which survived into the age of the camera, was the pinkie, a small double-ended vessel with an eighteenth century ancestry, used a great deal in the New England fishery but with close relatives in Canada. This pinkie, which came from Friendship in Maine, was typical, with her crew of three and the tubs of line on her deck. As with most New England fishing schooners before 1860 or so, fishing from this vessel was probably carried out from the deck, rather than over a wider area from boats dropped over the side. Notice how simple the rigging is, yet these little pinkies were safe and seaworthy vessels which, though small and slow, could and did survive very bad weather indeed.

110 This fine schooner is the mackerel seiner *Mabel Dilloway*, photographed in 1882. She carried a great seine-net boat, rather like a smaller version of an American whale boat, on her deck. Once on the fishing grounds the boat was launched, loaded with nets and towed astern of the schooner while a masthead man, clearly visible in this photograph, kept a look out for evidence of mackerel. When fish were sighted an attempt was made to encircle the shoal with the great seine net. The net was then pursed in and brought alongside the schooner and the fish baled out with smaller nets onto the schooner's deck. They were split and salted on board the schooner and the crews would frequently work all night when they were on a good run of fish.

111 Another classic type of American and Canadian fishing schooner which developed at the very end of the history of sailing fishing vessels was the 'Indian Header', yachtlike in general appearance but with a very lofty working schooner rig. These vessels were among the most handsome and efficient for their purpose of all working sailing ships. Their shape is shown very well in this photograph of one of the finest of them, the *Elsie* built at Essex, Massachusetts, in 1910. Essex was the birthplace of this type of schooner and the *Elsie* is shown under repair on one of the local builder's slipways. These vessels fished by dropping their flat-bottomed dories, carried nested inside one another on deck when they were not actually in use, over the side. From each dory two men fished with long lines, carrying many hundreds of baited hooks. In this way the fishing area of each vessel was greatly extended. But it was a rigorous and dangerous way of earning a living, brilliantly described in Rudyard Kipling's classic of the Gloucester fishery *Captains Courageous*. Two of these schooners have been preserved and can be seen today, the *L. A. Dunton* at Mystic Seaport and the *Theresa O. Connor* at Lunenberg, Nova Scotia. A replica of another, the famous Canadian schooner *Bluenose*, was built in the early 1960s and at the time of writing is still sailing from Halifax, Nova Scotia.

112   British drift-net fishing in the days of sail—as opposed to dragging a trawl net—was done mainly from lug-rigged boats using sails of a type which did not develop at all in North America. This photograph shows a St Ives drifter sailing in company with a pretty Norwegian brig, a merchant ship of the type which brought timber from Scandinavia to Britain in great quantities in the late nineteenth century. This St Ives boat fished by laying a curtain of net astern of her in the water with floats on top of it and weights on the lower edge. The drifter lay head to the sea with the nets stretched out behind her and her men hoped that they would prove to be in the path of shoals of herring and other fish, which were caught by becoming entangled by the gills. When the net was hauled in each fish had to be laboriously removed separately.

113 The British inshore fishery was conducted in smaller boats, again usually lug-rigged, at least in the latter part of the nineteenth century, the era of the camera. This very handsome vessel is the *Alaska*, a Cornish crabber from Sennen Cover near Land's End, photographed when her crew were fishing for mackerel with lines in Mounts Bay. In boats like this, thousands of men scraped a living in the late nineteenth century and before the First World War, in different fisheries all around the coasts of Britain. The lives of these beach fishermen and their families were described brilliantly by Stephen Reynolds, a young writer who settled at Sidmouth in South Devon and was assimilated into the local community. He takes the reader into the very roots of the life, telling of what the continuous poverty meant, and the hardships, both of the families at home and the fishermen in the boats. Notice, for instance, that although this boat will often be out all night she has no protection against the weather for her crew.

114 Compare the *Alaska* with her American equivalent, a lobster boat of about the same size. She has two spritsails in place of the lugs, is lower in the water and sharper of hull and is steered with an oar as she sails across the harbour at Portland, Maine. This particular type was known as a Hampton boat and this was one of the few North American inshore fishing boats built lapstrake or clinker with the planks overlapping at the edges. Most British fishing boats were built in this way.

115 This splendid photograph shows a most interesting boat coming ashore in the Magdalene Islands in the Gulf of St Lawrence, where she belonged. She is a big dory of a special local kind rigged as a two-masted boat or shallop—an early form of schooner much used in the eighteenth century. She is about to unload her catch of fish into the two-wheeled cart which has come down for the purpose. This fishing was evidently a family operation off the beach and, as in Britain at the same period at the end of the last century, the handling of the fish once they were ashore was evidently the job of the womenfolk who have come down with the cart. Apart from the style of dress, this scene is unchanged from the eighteenth or even the seventeenth centuries. Even the boat herself represents an early form of the dory still so common in every New England fishing harbour and on the Atlantic coasts of France and Portugal from which it came to North America.

116   Fishing for salmon and other fish with a seine net secured at one end to a sandy shore and spilled out over the stern of a boat rowed in a wide arc and back to the shore, then gradually pulled in, was used widely in different parts of Britain and North America. These men are loading back into the boat a net which has already been used for one cast. They are salmon fishermen photographed in North Devon at the very beginning of this century. Their long, narrow, strong, clinker-built boats, able to carry the load of the wet net and yet easy to row, are very characteristic of this type of fishery in Britain.

117   These men are fishing for menhaden in Nar-ragansett Bay, Rhode Island, about the year 1900. This too is a net fishery, like that illustrated in the last photograph, but of a totally different kind, as are the boats. Here the men are using a seine oper-ated from a pair of boats, one a big seaworthy double ender and the other a beamy flat-bottomed boat. Both these boats are characteristically North American. Flat-bottomed boats of the type used by the two men on the right scarcely occurred as working boats in Britain at all. These menha-den fishermen are fortunate; from the flurry of water in the net it looks as though they have a reasonably good catch.

Yachting

118 In the late nineteenth century and until the First World War yachting on both sides of the Atlantic was in the heyday of the period of the big sailing yachts and steam yachts. This photograph of a regatta scene at Marblehead, Massachusetts, in 1902 illustrates the point very well. The forest of masts in the background represents a mass of big vessels, mostly schooners seventy or eighty feet long. The catboats and sloops in the foreground are nearer to the size of the mass of modern yachts. No quayside camera anywhere in the world is likely to record a sight like this again. Notice the sun covers on the catboats nearest the camera, with their scalloped edges, reminiscent again of the 'Surrey with the fringe on top'.

119 Here is a somewhat similar scene in England taken at Dartmouth in South Devon in 1886. Here the yachts are of a different type. Though the rig never became really fashionable in England there are several schooners; the ketch, which took the schooner's place in the English yachting scene, is illustrated with half a dozen examples and there are two steam yachts in the foreground, one of them not more than twenty feet long. The brigs are part of the Naval training fleet of the period, very handsome little vessels which in the end became the last representatives of sail in the Royal Navy. Notice the boat's crew coming alongside the brig on the lefthand side of the picture with their oars tossed in Naval fashion.

120   The smart little sloop is the *Fiddler* (E 11) an American day-boat raced in New England waters by a pioneer yachts-woman, Miss Caroline Dabney, who had an all-woman crew known at the time as 'the Petti-coat Crew'. The photograph was taken between 1901 and 1902 and the woman who appears to be clearing the weather staysail sheet, her ankle length skirt wrapping itself around the mast behind her, would seem to be in some peril if Miss Dabney has to luff up.

121   These yachts on Lake Windermere, photographed in the 1890s, are comparable in size with Miss Dabney's, but of a much more old-fashioned type with their straight stems and long stern overhangs. They were narrow and deep and their picturesque rig with its jackyard, gaff topsails and enormous jibs on bowsprits was, of course, far less handy. The yachts belonged to members of the Royal Windermere Yacht Club, founded in 1889. The regular course for their races was from the ferry at Bowness up to the top of the town then back down to the south end of the Lake and back to the town, about ten miles of sailing.

122   The annual regatta at the town of Calstock in Cornwall was a great event in the 1890s, as it still is today. This photograph shows the start of a rowing race; the town is still famous for its oarsmen and oarswomen. The coasting smack with flags in use as a committee boat is the *Britannia* locally built and owned. Notice the country fair on the quay behind. There is a steam roundabout or carousel immediately behind the *Britannia's* mast which, judging from the crowd, is likely to get plenty of custom later in the day.

123   This photograph also shows a rowing race, but on the Kennebunk River at Kennebunkport, Maine. The contrast with the boats in the last photograph is noticeable. Those at Calstock are all clinker-built, rather flat-sheered, heavy boats meant for use on a tidal river. Those on the Kennebunk are more elegant, lighter in construction and designed solely for pleasure rowing with passengers, a number of them have what would have been called at the time 'lady oarsmen'. It seems likely that there is no actual race taking place in this photograph but that the assemblage of boats has gathered together on this hot summer's day to watch the finish when the boats arrive.

124   This big steel schooner is being launched at the yard of the Gas Engine & Power Company and Charles L. Seabury & Co, Consolidated, Morris Heights, Harlem, New York City. The crowd is evidently still assembling and the sun shades show it is a blazing hot day. The launch of a yacht this size nowadays would be a major occasion. At this period, probably the 1890s, it was a much more everyday affair. There are two big steam yachts in the background of the photograph apparently undergoing refitting.

125   This is a launch of a very different kind, a beach pleasure boat photographed at a seaside resort in Britain early in the present century. Passenger trips in boats like this were a great feature of seaside holidays in the nineteenth century and until the First World War. Sometimes the boats were local fishing craft, temporarily serving with passengers, but often at the regular resorts they were specially built for the purpose. They usually lay in the surf between trips with passengers. This one is probably awaiting the rapidly rising tide and she will make her first trip when she can be conveniently launched off the shingle bank on which she lies. Boats like this have their modern equivalent, but it is difficult to believe that the motorboats which carry passengers today give quite the same satisfaction as the adventure of a sail in one of these little working ships must have done, and all for two shillings for perhaps an hour's sailing.

Wrecks

126   This grim photograph shows a vessel which has been a brig or a brigantine ashore in heavy surf on a shallow part of the British coast. The gale is still blowing and the tops are being torn off the breakers as they come ashore—notice the wall of water coming in beyond the brigantine's bows—there is spray flying everywhere. The vessel is a total loss, shattered like a crashed aeroplane. From the fact that both boats appear to be still on board it is likely that the vessel went ashore at high tide and that the crew, as sometimes happened in such cases, were able to survive on board until the tide left their vessel high and dry, and then to walk ashore across the sands.

The wooden sailing ship was probably the most dangerous vehicle ever developed by man and the losses, particularly of small sailing vessels in the coastal trades and fishing fleets on both sides of the Atlantic, were appalling by modern standards.

128 (opposite)   This fine wooden full-rigged ship is the *Golden State*, ashore at Cape Elizabeth, Portland, Maine, in December 1866. She was built by J. A. Westervelt at New York in 1853. The *Golden State* was a great clipper in her day, among other things famous for a voyage in 1855 when she sailed under Captain Ranlett from New York in company with the *Golden Fleece* on 22 June. Both vessels entered the port of San Francisco only a few hours apart on 29 October, 129 days out.

127 This photograph shows the pretty little brigantine *Lady Napier*, built at Georgetown, Prince Edward Island, Canada, in 1902 registered at Charlottetown in the Island and owned in St John's, Newfoundland. She is ashore at Sandy Hook, New York, in 1907. The sea is moderate and she does not appear much damaged. It is likely she came ashore in fog and was salved for she continued sailing until 1911.

129   There is a tendency nowadays to think of all sailing ships as splendid seaworthy craft. Of course the very reverse was true. Standards of strength of construction and maintenance were gradually imposed during the latter part of the nineteenth century, but even at its end many old vessels were still around on both sides of the Atlantic which would now be considered completely unfit to go to sea. It was normal for the leaks in old wooden ships to be so bad that the crew had to pump more or less continuously, and a vessel with obvious damage could continue carrying cargoes for months on end. The circumstances in which this photograph of a brigantine from Maryport (her name cannot be read) was taken are not known, but with damage to her stern and rudder and with water pouring in a steady stream out of one of her bilge seams, she is by no means untypical of the state in which many vessels continued to trade for years before the gradual extension of safety requirements imposed both by Governments and insurers on both sides of the Atlantic made it impossible for people to earn their living with them any longer.

Warships

130   A quayside camera in the 1880s could still photograph a three-decker of the Napoleonic Wars afloat and fully rigged, if not in a seagoing state. This one was the *St Vincent*, laid down at Devonport in 1810, Flagship at Portsmouth from 1841 to 1848 and at sea as a transport during the Crimean War in 1854. She then became a boys' training ship at Portsmouth and it was in this capacity that she was serving when photographed. She was broken up in 1906.

131　During the age of the camera the British Navy changed from one entirely comprising vessels like the *St Vincent* to a great force of steel steamships. Enormous technical changes in armaments, gunnery, communications and organisation took place at the same time. The western world, and in particular the United States, could develop relatively peaceably behind the protection given by the presence of this great modern navy and was saved the great expense of maintaining similar forces. The much smaller United States Navy went through a similar process of change and this photograph well illustrates one of the intermediate stages, that of the 'steam and sail' navy. The vessel is the USS *Brooklyn*, built at New York in 1858 and commissioned in 1859 under Captain David G. Farragut. She played an active part in the war between the states and continued in service until 1889, shortly after this photograph was taken at a naval review. The photograph shows a spectacular practice common in the days when warships still had masts and yards and sails, that of 'manning the yards'. It depended on the presence of a wire stay stretched above the yard behind the men, to which they are holding with their outstretched arms.

132   This photograph shows the next stage, the Navy as steel and steam without sails. The vessel is the second class cruiser *Melampus* and she was one of numerous small cruisers built under the Naval Defence Act of 1889. She lasted for twenty years and saw no war service, being broken up in 1910.

133   The vessel on the right is the British third class cruiser *Pelorus* built in 1896. She was commissioned with the Channel fleet from 1897 to 1901, then she was on the Cape Station in South Africa. Her final peacetime commission was from 1912 to 1914 on the East Indies station, largely in the Persian Gulf. She survived the First World War, which she spent in the Mediterranean. The other vessel is the *Gossamer*, a torpedo gunboat, but because she was too slow to catch torpedo boats she was converted to be a minesweeper. She also survived the First World War.

134   This pleasant little scene shows the brigantine-rigged training ship built upon the hull of an old London river sailing barge which was established by the Windsor and Eton branch of the Navy League in 1899, with some of her cadets. The lads are obviously keen and smart with their miniature old-fashioned seaman's uniforms, the field gun and ammunition and the stretcher party behind. One of the lads has paraded on crutches. The photograph, which must have been taken shortly before the outbreak of war in Europe in 1914, will serve well to end this book on a happy note, for most of the lads appear to be young enough to escape the coming holocaust. But they would grow up into a sea world, both in the Navy and in merchant shipping, utterly different from that illustrated in this volume.

Index

112